NO FREEZE IN BREEZE

A Compilation of Poems in My Life's Journey

SAYO AKINTOLA

COVENANT PUBLISHING

No Freeze In Breeze: A Compilation of Poems in My Life's Journey by Sayo Akintola

Unless otherwise indicated, all Scripture quotations are taken from New King James Version (NKJV) of the Bible.

ISBN 978-1-907734-5-64
First Edition, April 2025

Cover Design by Covenant Publishing Team
Published by Covenant Publishing
Printed in the United Kingdom

TABLE OF CONTENTS

Dedication

I wholeheartedly dedicate this book to the incredible women who have shaped my life with their love, wisdom, and unwavering support.

To My Mothers:

- Mama Olatundun Eyinlola Akintola
- Mama Olayinka Wuraola Amodu
- Mama Beatrice Foyeke Ajagbe
- Mama Tinuade Olayemi Mould

Each of you has played a profound role in moulding me into the person I am today. Your strength, sacrifices, prayers, and guidance have been the steady winds that have propelled me forward, ensuring that no storm could freeze my purpose or halt my journey.

This book stands as a testament to the resilience, courage, and faith you instilled in me. May your legacy of love and wisdom continue to inspire generations to come.

Acknowledgment

My deepest gratitude goes to God, who has been exceedingly gracious to me – granting me life, sound health, and countless blessings. Even in times when I could not boast of knowing Him, His goodness never wavered.

I have often highlighted that while some people are born with silver or golden spoons in their mouths, my story was one of having no spoon at all. I was raised from the lowest of the low, yet looking back, I can only give thanks to God, whom I encountered at the age of seventeen. It was on a Sunday morning in April 1983, at St. Peter's Anglican Church, Aremo, Ibadan, Nigeria, through the preaching of Pastor Omololu Adegoke. That encounter changed the course of my life completely.

This book is a product of my many life experiences – an extraordinary journey marked by deep valleys and soaring peaks. It has been a tapestry of woven intricacies, and my goal is not to present myself as a poet, but as someone who transforms personal stories into something meaningful – something others can draw strength from. If you look closely, you will see pains, struggles, and victories, depending on your perspective.

I would like to acknowledge my biological children, who initially doubted my ability to compose poetry. What they did not realize was that their scepticism became an impetus for me to try. Before long, they became my greatest fans and encouragers. Thank you, Marvey. Thank you, David.

I am immensely grateful to my beloved daughter in the Lord, Mrs. Kemi Emmanuel, whose unwavering support was invaluable. Despite her busy schedule, she took the time to read, edit, and even type out my handwritten poems – often deciphering my less-than-perfect handwriting. Thank you, my dear.

To my dear son and friend, Chime Emmanuel Okoli, how can I quantify your contributions? You were like an angel – tirelessly typing, straining over details, and offering constructive feedback that pushed me beyond my limits. May God reward you abundantly.

This project received a significant boost when my beautiful daughter, Grace Dabiara Ojo, got involved. At just thirteen years old, she worked like a seasoned editor, pouring immense effort into this work. Grace, your contributions were monumental, and without you, I wonder how far this would have come.

A special thank you to Revd. Olufemi Oyelade, my brother, friend, and mentor. Your kindness in writing the foreword means the world to me. May you continue to enjoy the abundant blessings of God.

To Pastor Tosin and Titi Williams, I am deeply grateful for your support.

My profound appreciation goes to my General Overseer, Revd. and Mrs. Paul Jinadu – I owe you so much. Thank you also to Revd. and Mrs. Emmanuel Olasupo Ajao, true mentors in every sense.

To Revd. Dr. and Prof. Soetan, your friendship means a great deal to me and my family.

Foreword

I have known Rev Sayo Akintola for about two decades as a beloved brother and co-worker in God's vineyard. From his base in London, UK, he serves as an International Pastor in the New Covenant Church and has been used of God to plant many branches of the church in different parts of the world.

"No Freeze In Breeze" is poetic and motivational, offering hope and encouragement. At the end of each chapter, relevant Questions for Reflections; and in some cases, Prayer Points are presented.

In a down-to-earth fashion, the author, illustrating from his own experience asked, " Have you noticed that problems rarely come alone? They seem to arrive in multitudes, with new challenges emerging before the previous ones are resolved."

The experience of a leader, whether at home, at work, in the church or in the larger society, is aptly captured in a poem in the chapter, "Sun, Please Don't Shine." According to the author, "This poem springs from a deep pain felt by those who pour their hearts into bringing joy to others. Often, the beneficiaries of these efforts remain oblivious to the sacrifices involved."

In times of challenges, the author recommends some steps including Silence, Joy and Action.

According to him, "Silence allows us to weigh our thoughts and emotions, offering clarity in the midst of chaos. Silence is golden. It can provide space for introspection and peace, offering wisdom that words cannot convey."

Drawing lessons from other creatures he poetically stresses the importance or rejoicing in tribulation:

The bird sings even when caged
But never wished for the cage
Let it out today, and your fear might end
There is strength in freedom.
There is "no freeze in breeze"

Asking readers not to freeze in the face of breeze of challenges, he urged readers to keep on keeping on,

To ride a bicycle, like a circle
Moving as you press the pedals
Strength is needed to keep pushing
Rusty and hard at first
But every push softens the wheel
Turning effort into smooth motion

He pins his basis of encouragement and motivation on the scriptures and this I strongly reinforce, as Paul the Apostle enjoins believers to in Romans 11:12:

Rejoice in hope
Be patient in tribulation
Continuing steadfastly in prayer

I commend this book to the reader with hope and prayer that the Lord will use it to strengthen you during trials and help you not to freeze in the face of breeze.

Rev. Olufemi Oyelade
Deputy General Overseer
New Covenant Church

Introduction

Life is a journey of seasons – some filled with clarity, others clouded with uncertainty. At times, we stand firm, confident in our steps, while at other times, we are swept into storms that shake our very foundation. The winds of life do not always blow in our favour; they can be gentle, carrying us forward with ease, or they can be fierce, pushing against us with unrelenting force. Yet, the greatest test is not in the strength of the wind but in our response to it. Will we freeze in fear, immobilised by hardship, or will we allow the breeze – whether strong or subtle – to propel us forward into our God-ordained purpose?

This book, "No Freeze In Breeze", is a reflection of that journey. It captures moments of struggle, resilience, transformation, and hope. Each poem tells a story – some born out of deep pain, others inspired by faith's triumph over adversity. These are not just words; they are echoes of real-life experiences, of battles fought in silence, of questions whispered in the dark, and of victories won in the dawn of a new day.

A Journey Through Life's Winds

The journey begins with A Season of Sight / Am Partially Blind, where vision is clouded, and understanding is incomplete. It is the season where life presents more questions than answers, and the path ahead seems uncertain. The World Changed Me reflects on how life's experiences shape us – sometimes for the better, sometimes in ways we never anticipated.

Then comes the cry of Sun, Please Don't Shine, a plea from the heart that has seen too much and longs for refuge from the harshness of reality. Trap Dream speaks of those moments when we chase illusions, believing in a false sense of hope, only to find ourselves ensnared by disappointment. Life, in its unpredictability, often throws unexpected trials our way, much like The Pigeon Pooed – a seemingly minor yet frustrating misfortune that reminds us of how little we control.

In Rolling the Dice, we confront the risks we take, the leaps of faith, and the uncertainty of outcomes. But amid these struggles, we find moments of self-realisation, like in I Am Not Guilty, where one comes to terms with their past, their mistakes, and the grace that declares them free. Yet, even in those moments, we sometimes encounter The King's Silence, where God seems distant, and the heavens remain quiet despite our desperate prayers.

Embracing Change and Finding Hope

But life is not just about storms; it is also about learning new rhythms. The New Dance signifies a shift – a willingness to adapt, to move with grace despite the uncertainties. No Freeze in Breeze, the very heart of this book, is a declaration that we will not be paralyzed by adversity but will continue to press forward, no matter how fierce the winds may be.

Then comes the inevitable question: When Can I Finally Say: "It Is Well"? This question lingers in the hearts of those who have endured, who have fought long battles and still await their moment of peace. Yet, the answer does come – first in A New Day, where light breaks through the darkness, and finally in Happy Days Are Here to Stay, a testimony to restoration, renewal, and the joy that lasts.

Why This Book Matters

No Freeze in Breeze is more than a collection of poems – it is an invitation to reflect on your own journey. It is for those who have felt stuck, unsure of their next step. It is for those who have battled storms that threatened to break them. It is for those who have questioned their purpose and wondered if hope still exists.

My prayer is that as you turn these pages, you will find encouragement, strength, and the unwavering truth that no storm lasts forever. The wind may blow, the road may be uncertain, but you do not have to freeze in fear or despair. Instead, you can lean into the breeze, trust in the One who holds the winds in His hands and move forward with courage.

Welcome to No Freeze in Breeze. May these words bring you light, warmth, and the strength to keep moving.

A Season of Sight: I am Partially Blind

Is it true that I am partially blind?
Though my eyes are open, do they grasp the whole truth?
I see the surface – the shapes, the shadows, the outlines
But is that enough
As I pause, letting the moment settle in my mind
I realize sight alone cannot capture the depths.
There's always more beyond the visible
Hidden layers waiting for patient eyes to find
The picture sharpens, edges soften
Thank God for the panoramic lens
That reveals angles I once ignored
Perspectives hidden in the periphery
What once seemed complete
Was only a fragment, a sliver of the whole
Now, with broader sight
I see the intricate tapestry of truth
Threads woven from viewpoints beyond my own
My judgment was not flawed
It was simply incomplete
What I saw was true
But truth is vast, multifaceted
And my lens captured just a portion

So, I lower my guard
Open my heart to the unseen
For wisdom whispers in humility's ear
Knowledge is a vast ocean
And I have only dipped my toes
Listen to the cock's crow at dawn
A herald of new beginnings
And to the bull's steady breath
Rooted, grounded, unwavering
Even in their simplicity
They speak truths I might have missed
Sometimes, it's not the loudest voice
But the quietest whisper
That holds the key to understanding
It is in silence, not speech
That clarity often blooms
In every message lies a mess
Tangled threads of mistakes and missteps
But as time unfolds – age lending its patience
The chaos begins to make sense
It takes a sage, one tempered by trials
To sift through the mess

To find the lessons hidden in the debris
A message isn't born from perfection
But from the struggle
The journey from confusion to clarity
From brokenness to meaning
Don't fight the lessons life brings
Let them shape you
Like rivers carve valleys over time
This is your season of wisdom
A time to listen, to see, to grow
For every challenge is a teacher
And every struggle holds a seed
A seed that, when nurtured with patience
Will bloom into understanding

A Season of Sight: I Am Partially Blind

One of the greatest tools for navigating life is the weapon of humility. Humility, as defined by Oxford Languages, is quality of having a modest or low view of one's importance.

The Cambridge Dictionary expands on this by describing humility as quality of being modest or respectful in one's self-assessment and behaviour. It involves recognizing and accepting one's limitations, valuing other people's contributions, and maintaining a sense of perspective.

Sadly, many people myself included have been guilty of pride, arrogance, or rudeness without even realizing it. This unchecked attitude can be both damaging and destructive, hindering personal growth and the ability to relate well with others.

It is now clearer why the Bible gives this wise counsel:

"Understand this, my beloved brothers and sisters. Let everyone be quick to hear [be a careful, thoughtful listener], slow to speak [a speaker of carefully chosen words], slow to anger [patient, reflective, forgiving] (James 1:19, AMP).

No one has a monopoly on wisdom. The ability to listen to others and consider different perspectives is essential before making final judgments on matters of importance.

There is an old story that illustrates this well.

A group of people was asked to describe an elephant. Some were fascinated by its trunk, others by its massive size, and yet others by its tusks. Though their descriptions were different, each one was true in its own way. It would have been entirely unfair to claim that only one of them had the correct description of the elephant while dismissing the rest.

Even in a court of law, no matter how compelling the accusations of the plaintiff may seem, the court still allows the accused to present a defence. Wisdom is not found in silencing others, even when their views challenge or contradict our own.

The Limitations of Human Knowledge

One of the many branches of philosophy is "epistemology" which is the study of knowledge. Within this field, there is a discussion on revelation, which highlights an important reality: Two people can sleep on the same bed and have completely different dreams. It would be unfair for one person to insist that their dream is more significant or valid than the others.

Every experience carries its own unique lessons, and wisdom comes from being open to learning at every stage of life. As someone once said, "The day you stop learning is the day you start dying".

Knowledge makes life easier to navigate.

A Lesson in Wisdom

Let me conclude with a story I once heard. A young man was searching for employment. He had an impressive resume and was highly intelligent, but he lacked wisdom. Whenever he attended job interviews, he was punctual and enthusiastic.

However, when asked a question, he would provide both relevant and irrelevant answers, assuming that speaking more would impress the interview panel.

Unfortunately, this habit often cost him the opportunity to advance to the next stage of the interview process.

After several failed attempts, a friend advised him to focus only on answering the specific questions asked and to eliminate unnecessary details. He took the advice to heart, and not long after, he secured his dream job.

This experience taught him a valuable lesson: sometimes, silence is golden.

The World Changed Me

I wanted to change the world; I believed I could
Positive and committed, I set out with high hopes
But alas! Looking back now, the world has changed me instead
A strong man like me will never concede victory
Yet perhaps, for once, I discovered my true strength
The preacher's words now make sense:
"Vanity upon vanity, all is vanity."
Is it true that zero times a million is still zero?
Why is zero so powerful, turning even billions into nothing?
I found the Songs of Solomon in the holy book
Freely speaking of breasts and love
Revealing the true strength of zero
I heard a strong cry that the Holy Book is incomplete
If it does not represent reality
Reality! Reality! Sincerely, it's tough
The word connotes strength, resistance, and pride
I conclude now: only a miracle can change reality
What we see has been
What will happen is nothing new
The same reality persists

I am not pessimistic

nor am I negative

It's just my experience with reality

That has taken the better part of me

The World Changed Me

It is unfortunate that the grass always seems greener on the other side. Life often appears simpler than it is. I've come to realise that we sometimes overestimate our potential and abilities. While motivational speakers encourage us to aim high and stay positive, it's crucial to balance this optimism with a realistic assessment of our true strengths and limitations. This helps prevent us from taking on more than we can handle.

In today's world, we often boast about our strengths and achievements. Many of us sincerely set out to accomplish our dreams, but unforeseen challenges can make it impossible to achieve our goals. Politicians, for instance, often make grand promises during elections, genuinely intending to fulfil them. However, many end up disappointing their followers due to challenges beyond their control.

A clear example of this was the global battle against COVID-19. The pandemic caught the world off guard, and we are still dealing with its aftermath. Sometimes, people may wrongly accuse you of things beyond your control, things you could never have anticipated.

A modern philosopher once said that the only constant in life is change. Therefore, change is inevitable. Sincerity may not always be enough to prove innocence, as time and circumstances often reveal our true nature. I've been humbled many times when I sincerely set out to achieve something, only to fall short of my promises.

One incident that stands out is the story of Peter, the disciple of Jesus. In Matthew 26:31-35 (NKJV), we read:

"Then Jesus said to them, "All of you will be made to stumble because of Me this night, for it is written: 'I will strike the Shepherd, And the sheep of the flock will be scattered.' But after I have been raised, I will go before you to Galilee." Peter answered and said to Him, "Even if all are made to stumble because of You, I will never be made to stumble." Jesus said to him, "Assuredly, I say to you that this night, before the rooster crows, you will deny Me three times." Peter said to Him, "Even if I have to die with You, I will not deny You!"

And so, said all the disciples. The gospels of Matthew, Luke, and John all record this prediction, highlighting Peter's confidence and sincerity. Jesus understood Peter's good intentions and prayed for his strength in Luke 22:33-34.

However, when faced with the reality of Jesus' arrest and torture, Peter's true strength was revealed. Overwhelmed, Peter denied Jesus three times, as described in Luke 22:55-62: And when they had kindled a fire in the middle of the courtyard and sat down together, Peter sat down among them. Then a servant girl, seeing him as he sat in the light and looking closely at him, said, "This man also was with him." But he denied it, saying, "Woman, I do not know him." And a little later someone else saw him and said, "You also are one of them." But Peter said, "Man, I am not." And after an interval of about an hour still another insisted, saying, "Certainly this man also was with him, for he too is a Galilean." But Peter said, "Man, I do not know what you are talking about." And immediately, while he was still speaking, the rooster crowed. And the Lord turned and looked at Peter. And Peter remembered the saying of the Lord, how he had said to him, "Before the rooster crows today, you will deny me three times." And he went out and wept bitterly. Was Peter sincere? Yes. Was he prepared? No. The arrest and torture of Jesus were beyond his imagination, making it impossible for him to keep his promises.

I am learning never to say never in my journey in life.

Sun, Please Don't Shine

Sun, can I beg you, just for today – don't shine
Yes, don't shine, because when you do
It's bright and beautiful, but nobody sees
The burning, the pain, and the sweat
They ask me, "Why do you sweat so much?"
I'm confused and upset, because no one notices
The obvious. So many people, in so many places
Desire to see you beam from the sky
If only they could feel the pain
That accompanies your appearance
The pressure is immense
Felt only when you stand directly under it
You think I complain a lot
Because you appreciate the brightness
That comes with the Sun
Why wouldn't you get angry with me?
You're standing under a roof to enjoy the Sun
Would you be so happy If you were truly the roof?
You wonder why my skin suffers
Burning but glowing, darkening my body
Sun, it's just one day I ask for
But since you won't grant my request

Teach me how to cope

When you shine at your fullest strength

I rest my case

Sun, shine and keep on shining

But remember, even the brightest light can cast the darkest shadow

Sun, Please Don't Shine

Looking at this poem, it springs from a deep pain felt by those who pour their hearts into bringing joy to others. Often, the beneficiaries of these efforts remain oblivious to the sacrifices involved. The pressure to shine comes with a cost. Are you a star? People look up to you, many desiring the limelight, but anyone who has been there knows it is no easy journey.

I have been a pastor for most of my life, and many times when I preach, people fail to realize the amount of effort behind those messages. Speaking for 30 minutes to an hour without being boring is a major task. There are times after preaching when I know I haven't done justice to the assignment, yet people around me may lack the confidence to tell me the truth, not wanting to hurt my feelings. Despite knowing the truth myself, I am my harshest critic, which explains why I don't like to listen to my sermons after preaching. The pressure to do well is immense, placing heavy demands on you. As a preacher, whenever your name is mentioned, there is an expectation from the audience. You don't want to let them down, which adds to the pressure.

Many of us occupy positions that others envy, but they fail to see the price we pay to maintain those roles, which can be demanding and painful.

Consider the story of Princess Diana and her interactions with the press. It was terrifying how they invaded her private life, forcing her to employ private guards and use every trick to evade the cameras. The glamorous lives of superstars come with the heavy burden of constant scrutiny.

David's struggle in the Bible provides a profound example. Fighting an external enemy is one thing, but when the battle is with your own blood – your son, Absalom – It is much more challenging. In 2 Samuel 15:1-6, Absalom led an open revolt against his father:

"After this it happened that Absalom provided himself with chariots and horses, and fifty men to run before him. Now Absalom would rise early and stand beside the way to the gate. So it was, whenever anyone who had a lawsuit came to the king for a decision, that Absalom would call to him and say, 'What city are you from?' And he would say, 'Your servant is from such and such a tribe of Israel.' Then Absalom would say to him, 'Look, your case is good and right; but there is no deputy of the king to hear you.' Moreover, Absalom would say, 'Oh, that I were made judge in the land, and everyone who has any suit or cause would come to me; then I would give him justice.' And so, it was, whenever anyone came near to bow down to him, that he would put out his hand and take him and kiss him. In this manner, Absalom acted toward all Israel who came to the king for judgment. So, Absalom stole the hearts of the men of Israel."

How do you handle such a challenging fight? Do you abdicate the truth for your son or engage in open battle with him? The situation grew dire in 2 Samuel 15:13 when David had to flee for his life – not from a stranger, but from his own son. David was a man after God's heart (1 Samuel 13:14), anointed as king without his consent. Imagine his struggles: fleeing from King Saul, living in trenches, and hiding – not because he did wrong, but because of unnecessary jealousy. Saul wasted time pursuing innocent David instead of fighting the Philistines.

Fighting external enemies was one thing, but battling within his family was another. As Absalom's conspiracy grew stronger, David was advised to vacate to save his life. The depth of his problem was evident when Shimei cursed him on his way out of the city (2 Samuel 16:5-13).

David was surrounded by mighty men, but this was not a conventional battle. He was wrongly accused, spat at, and called names because his son rose against him. David's response to Abishai, who wanted to silence Shimei, shows his deep understanding of his predicament.

In 2 Samuel 18:1-5, David prepared for inevitable war, commanding his captains to deal gently with Absalom. Despite all Absalom did, David couldn't curse him, seeing him as a young man unaware of his actions' consequences. When the battle was won and Absalom was killed, David mourned deeply (2 Samuel 18:29-33).

For Joab, the death of the prince was unavoidable, but for David, it was a mixture of emotions. He would have preferred to die in place of his son. David's story illustrates that sometimes, victory comes at too high a cost.

Joab captured the situation's depth when he threatened David with desertion if he didn't address the people (2 Samuel 19:7). David, despite his depression, had to muster the courage to inspire his followers – a heavy price of leadership.

The story of David and Absalom isn't unique. Judges 11:30-31 tells of Jephthah, who made a rash vow, resulting in his daughter's sacrifice on the day of his victory. Victory turned into mourning for his household.

Every leader need encouragement. Leaders, whether secular or religious, face their own challenges. On one particular Saturday, I received a call at midnight informing me that my son had been rushed to the hospital. Saturdays are usually for perfecting my Sunday messages and resting. Hearing this news late at night left me no room to call on my ministerial team to stand in for me. Early Sunday morning, we went to the hospital, but I had to leave my son with my wife to preach.

Despite the pain, I preached without letting the congregation know our predicament. Afterwards, when I mentioned it to a few leaders, one admitted he was getting angry at my unusual lateness but was relieved after hearing what I'd been through.

Can you imagine how many times we've judged our leaders unfairly, not considering what they might be going through?

The poem "Sun, Please Don't Shine" is for all leaders – secular, religious, or otherwise. Be encouraged, keep going, and may the Lord grant you strength.

Worksheet: Supporting and Encouraging Your Leaders

1. Send a Message of Appreciation
   - Write a heartfelt card or text message to your leader, expressing your gratitude for their dedication and hard work.
   - Mention specific instances where their leadership positively impacted you or others.
   - Highlight their qualities and efforts that you admire and appreciate.

Sample Message

"Dear [Leader's Name],

I want to take a moment to express my deep appreciation for all you do. Your dedication, wisdom, and compassion have been a guiding light for me and many others. I particularly remember [specific instance] when your leadership made a significant difference. Thank you for your unwavering commitment and the sacrifices you make to lead us so effectively.

With gratitude,

[Your Name]"

2. Offer Practical Support
    - Identify ways to help lighten your leader's load. This could be through volunteering for tasks, offering your skills, or providing resources.
    - Form a support group with others to share the responsibilities and provide consistent help.
    - Suggest practical solutions for any challenges you notice they face and offer to assist in implementing these solutions.

Ideas for Practical Support

- Volunteer to organize events or meetings.
- Offer administrative help, such as handling emails or scheduling.
- Provide technical assistance with presentations or online platforms.
- Assist with logistics, such as setting up venues or arranging transportation.

3. Pray for Them
    - Dedicate regular time to pray for your leaders, asking for strength, wisdom, and guidance in their roles.
    - Include specific prayer points such as health, family well-being, and clarity in decision-making.
    - Consider organizing a prayer group focused on supporting your leaders through collective prayer.

Sample Prayer

"Dear Lord,

We lift up our leader, [Leader's Name], to You today. Grant them the strength and wisdom they need to lead us effectively. Bless them with good health, peace, and joy in their personal life. Help them to feel Your presence and guidance in every decision they make. May they always find encouragement and support from those around them. Amen."

4. Avoid Unfair Judgments
    - Be mindful not to judge your leaders hastily. Recognize that they may be facing unseen challenges.
    - Seek to understand their perspectives and the pressures they endure.
    - Offer constructive feedback with empathy and kindness, focusing on solutions rather than criticism.
    - Steps to Avoid Unfair Judgments:
    - Take time to reflect before forming opinions about their actions.
    - Communicate openly and respectfully if you have concerns or suggestions.
    - Encourage a culture of understanding and patience within your community.

5. Express Public Support
    - Show your support for your leader publicly during meetings or gatherings.
    - Acknowledge their hard work and dedication in front of others to boost their morale.
    - Encourage others to do the same, creating a positive and supportive environment.
    - Ways to Express Public Support:
    - During meetings, take a moment to thank your leader for their efforts.
    - Write a public post on social media highlighting their achievements and expressing gratitude.
    - Organize a small event or appreciation day to celebrate their contributions.

By actively participating in these actions, you contribute to creating a nurturing and supportive environment for your leaders, helping them to thrive and continue their important work effectively.

Trap Dream

Is the dream worth dying for?

Or is it merely a trap, disguised in the allure of possibility

A mirage only I can see

To every bystander, it's shrouded in ambiguity

A distant, unreachable spectre

But to me, it's vibrant, alive, bursting with colour

A beacon of hope amidst the ordinary

I wonder, why is it that I alone perceive its brilliance

While others remain blind to its radiance?

I cannot convince you, cannot make you believe

In its reachability, its worth, its inevitable achievement

You dwell in the realm of the unbelievable

The unthinkable, the unbearable

But the key to understanding lies not within me

It lies within all who can glimpse what I've seen

Your doubts remind me of the statue of the Unknown Soldier

A monument to the forgotten, the nameless

Yet, I often ask myself: is the Soldier truly unknown?

To the families who lost a father, a brother

To the woman who lost her husband

That soldier was never unknown

His name may be lost to the world
But to those who loved him, he was everything
There are stories buried deep within the stone
Stories of valour, of sacrifice
Stories that will forever remain untold
I hope that when I finally meet this Unknown Soldier
When I stand before him and look into the depths of his silence
Everything will begin to make sense
I wrestle with this concept of the "unknown,"
For is anything truly unknown if we dare to unmask it?
Isn't it just hidden, waiting to be revealed?
Like coffee without its essence
Decaffeinated, diluted, drained of its power
So too does your disbelief sap the life from my dream
What was once bold and full of energy
Is now a shadow of its former self
A decaffeinated dream
Stripped of its strength
Deprived of its fire
Yet still, I hold onto it
Clinging to the hope that one day

It will regain its potency

That one day, you'll see it as I do

Not as a trap, but as a truth worth believing in and living for

Trap Dream

Introduction: The Power of Dreams

Where you find yourself today is, in many ways, a reflection of the dreams you've dared to dream in the past. It's tempting to attribute our current circumstances to external forces – circumstances, people, or even fate. However, upon deeper reflection, I've come to realise that the true source of our present reality often lies within ourselves: in the decisions we've made, the paths we've chosen, and the dreams we've allowed ourselves to believe in – or not.

Life is a journey fuelled by expectations and aspirations. It is only the living who are blessed with the gift of dreaming. A dead man has no dreams; his aspirations have perished with him. Yet, while dreaming is a natural part of life, believing in those dreams is a different matter entirely. The gap between a dream conceived and a dream realised is often wide and fraught with challenges.

The Nature of Dreams: Belief as the Catalyst

Dreams are a kind of knowledge, a revelation of what could be – a glimpse of potential that lies within us. In the realm of philosophy, particularly in epistemology, knowledge is a vast and complex topic. Dreams, however, are a unique form of knowledge – intensely personal, often difficult to articulate, and even harder for others to grasp. This is the crux of the dreamer's dilemma: how to hold fast to a vision that others cannot see.

Without a firm belief in your dream, it will struggle to survive. Conviction is the catalyst that turns a dream into a vision, and a vision into reality. Dreaming, then, is not merely an act of imagination; it is the beginning of a process that requires deep personal conviction. The first step is the grace to conceive the idea. But conception is only the beginning. The next, and perhaps the most crucial, step is to nurture that dream – to believe in it with every fibre of your being. Your conviction becomes the driving force that propels you forward, even when the road ahead is uncertain.

Communicating the Vision: Sharing and Defending the Dream.

To bring a dream to life, you must often communicate it to those around you, seeking their support and understanding. This is where the journey can become particularly challenging. As the prophet Habakkuk was instructed:

"Write the vision and make it plain on tablets, that he may run who reads it. For the vision is yet for an appointed time; but at the end it will speak, and it will not lie. Though it tarries, wait for it; because it will surely come, it will not tarry." (Habakkuk 2:2-3 NKJV)

Here, the scripture emphasises the importance of clarity and patience in pursuing a vision. Making the vision plain—communicating it clearly – is essential for garnering the support and momentum needed to realise it. Yet, even when the vision is clear, not everyone will understand it. Some may choose to ignore it, others may deny it, and still others may actively oppose it. These reactions can be deeply discouraging, especially when they come from those you hoped would support you.

It is in these moments of doubt and opposition that your conviction will be tested. You must be prepared to defend your vision, to hold fast to your dream even when it feels like the world is against you. This is the crucible in which true visionaries are forged.

The Challenge of Envy: Recognising the Dream Killers

There is a darker side to the journey of pursuing a dream, one that is often overlooked: the presence of those who seek to destroy what you are striving to build. These "dream killers" are not always those who disbelieve in your vision; sometimes, they are those who believe in it too much – so much so that they fear it. They see the potential in your dream and are threatened by it.

The story of Joseph is a poignant illustration of this. Joseph's brothers did not doubt the validity of his dreams; their concern was how to prevent them from becoming a reality. In their envy, they conspired to kill him, believing that by silencing the dreamer, they could extinguish the dream:

"Now when they saw him afar off, even before he came near them, they conspired against him to kill him. Then they said to one another, 'Look, this dreamer is coming! Come therefore, let us now kill him and cast him into some pit; and we shall say, 'Some wild beast has devoured him.' We shall see what will become of his dreams!'" (Genesis 37:18-20 NKJV)

Dream killers are those who, out of envy, fear, or spite, will do anything to ensure that your dream never sees the light of day. They may undermine you, sabotage your efforts, or, like Joseph's brothers, try to eliminate you entirely from the picture. The Resilience of the Dreamer: Overcoming Opposition When Joseph's brothers sold him into slavery, they thought they had rid themselves of both the dream and the dreamer. They believed that by removing Joseph from their lives, they had destroyed any possibility of his dreams coming true. How wrong they were!

As the story unfolds, Joseph's journey takes him from the depths of a pit to the heights of power in Egypt. Despite the many trials he faced – being sold into slavery, falsely accused, and imprisoned – Joseph's dream remained alive. Even in his darkest moments, the vision God had placed in his heart continued to guide him. When Joseph's brothers stood before him in Egypt, bowing down in the fulfilment of his dream, the truth became undeniable:

"Then his brothers also went and fell down before his face, and they said, 'Behold, we are your servants.'" (Genesis 50:18 NKJV).

What must have gone through Joseph's mind as he faced his brothers, now at his mercy? Here were the very people who had tried to destroy him, now bowing before him in recognition of the dream they had once sought to kill. The irony must have been overwhelming, but so too must have been the realisation that no matter what obstacles were placed in his path, the vision that God had given him would come to pass.

Conclusion: The Promise of the Dream

Joseph's story teaches us a profound lesson: a true dream, especially one inspired by God, cannot be thwarted by man. Though the journey may be long and fraught with challenges, though dream killers may arise, and opposition may seem insurmountable, the dream will find a way to come to pass.

The journey of a dream is not just about the destination; it's about the transformation that occurs along the way. It's about the resilience you build, the faith you cultivate, and the unwavering belief that what has been revealed to you in the quiet moments of your soul is worth every trial, every tear, and every test.

A dream is not merely a wish or a fleeting thought; it is a vision of what could be, a glimpse of a future that is yet to unfold. And though it may tarry, wait for it; because it will surely come, it will not tarry.

The power of a dream lies not just in its realisation, but in the journey of faith, perseverance, and transformation that it demands. Dream boldly, believe fiercely, and know that no matter the obstacles, your dream is a promise that, in due time, will flourish.

The Pigeon Pooed

I never once said you cannot poo

That is not what I am saying

But with all the vast expanse of sky

You chose my head as your target

I wouldn't have complained

If it were just one pigeon

But when many of you poo at once

It's hard to tell which poo smells the worst

I got so messed up and confused

You can poo, but please

Next time, be mindful of where

I am stronger and wiser now

I will shift my head

From the bullseye of your aim

Help, it smells so bad

But don't worry, it's temporary

I will no longer smell

I will become strong and clean up all your poos

It may take time, even years and months

Yes, I may need a new coat

For it's the brightness and colours

Of my beautiful coat that attract you

I've decided to change my coat

And guard myself against your whims

They say the lagoon is blue

But I realise its colour depends

On how far you are from the river

It's not always blue

Sometimes it's white

Depending on my attitude and altitude

Birds, you can poo, but please

For the sake of decency

Find another place next time

The Pigeon Pooed

Life can be unpredictable and challenging. Some of you may not have experienced much hardship yet, but for many of us, we've been battered, shattered, and bruised by life's events, often feeling helpless. This message is for those who have faced numerous challenges. I've often asked, "Why me?" and still struggle to find an answer. It feels like I am always the target of misunderstanding and worries.

Have you noticed that problems rarely come alone? They seem to arrive in multitudes, with new challenges emerging before the previous ones are resolved. Problems do not consider timing; they happen all at once, making it difficult to prioritise which to address first.

I remember a friend who was behind on his mortgage payments and struggling to avoid homelessness. During this time, he lost his job. As if that wasn't enough, he received news of his father's health challenges, requiring significant funds for treatment.

As a counsellor and pastor, it can be overwhelming to find the right words of comfort in such scenarios. The mortgage issue alone is significant without adding other problems. Sometimes, the question arises: why can't one problem wait for the right time to manifest? The answer is that it is a mystery, perhaps to be explained in the future.

The greatest strength for survival in life is hope. There are situations where you need to "believe in hope against hope," as stated in Romans 4:18. The Living Bible translation says, "Even when there was no reason for hope, Abraham kept hoping, believing..." This is challenging. Believing in hope against all odds means never allowing hope to die, no matter how daunting and challenging the circumstances.

Life is about making choices, often difficult ones. You can give up or stay strong. A friend of mine often says, "Tough times never last, but tough people do." This phrase, from Robert H. Schuller's book, is rich and comforting. It means you need to be tough to go through tough times. Before the pigeon can poo directly on your head, you must have been under the open sky, representing loneliness and reality. While dealing with a single incident of poo, another challenge is likely to arise, complicating an already difficult situation. Consider Hannah's story in 1 Samuel 1:1-13 (NKJV): "Now there was a certain man of Ramathaim Zophim, of the mountains of Ephraim, and his name was Elkanah the son of Jeroham, the son of Elihu, the son of Tohu, the son of Zuph, an Ephraimite. And he had two wives: the name of one was Hannah, and the name of the other Peninnah. Peninnah had children, but Hannah had no children. This man went up from his city yearly to worship and sacrifice to the Lord of hosts in Shiloh. Also, the two sons of Eli, Hophni and Phinehas, the priests of the Lord, were there.

And whenever the time came for Elkanah to make an offering, he would give portions to Peninnah his wife and to all her sons and daughters. But to Hannah, he would give a double portion, for he loved Hannah, although the Lord had closed her womb. And her rival also provoked her severely, to make her miserable, because the Lord had closed her womb. So it was, year by year, when she went up to the house of the Lord, that she provoked her; therefore, she wept and did not eat. Then Elkanah her husband said to her, 'Hannah, why do you weep? Why do you not eat? And why is your heart grieved? Am I not better to you than ten sons?' So, Hannah arose after they had finished eating and drinking in Shiloh. Now Eli the priest was sitting on the seat by the doorpost of the tabernacle of the Lord. And she was in bitterness of soul and prayed to the Lord and wept in anguish. Then she made a vow and said, 'O Lord of hosts, if You will indeed look on the affliction of Your maidservant and remember me, and not forget Your maidservant, but will give Your maidservant a male child, then I will give him to the Lord all the days of his life, and no razor shall come upon his head.' And it happened, as she continued praying before the Lord, that Eli watched her mouth. Now Hannah spoke in her heart; only her lips moved, but her voice was not heard. Therefore, Eli thought she was drunk. But Hannah answered and said, 'No, my Lord, I am a woman of sorrowful spirit. I have drunk neither wine nor intoxicating drink, but have poured out my soul before the Lord. Do not consider your maidservant a wicked woman, for out of the abundance of my complaint and grief I have spoken until now.' Then Eli answered and said, 'Go in peace, and the God of Israel grant your petition which you have asked of Him.' And she said, 'Let your maidservant find favor in your sight.' So, the woman went her way and ate, and her face was no longer sad." Let's highlight and analyse Hannah's journey to realising her dream. The narrative suggests Hannah was likely Elkanah's first wife, and her inability to conceive may have led him to marry Peninnah. The second wife easily bore many children while the Bible states, "the Lord had closed Hannah's womb." This raises the question: why? What had she done wrong? It is enough to be barren, but why would such trouble come from God?

Hannah's rival provoked her, adding insult to injury. While Hannah may have coped with this, the priest's misunderstanding and insult were the final straw. Many of us would break at this point. Why go to the temple when even the priest is blind, arrogant, and insulting? This was truly a test of Hannah's strength. If you were Hannah, what would your response be? In 2022 and 2023, I faced many losses within my family. My beloved dad died after a brief illness, and two weeks later, I lost my junior sister. The death of my father was a huge blow as we were very close, but my sister's death was even more painful. I couldn't cry because the pain was too deep. It felt like the whole world had crumbled. I was afraid, worried, and depressed, unable to explain my feelings to anyone. However, looking back, I thank God for His healing.

I used to think being a Christian meant escaping life's challenges. However, the story of Job teaches otherwise. Job was so depressed that he cursed the day of his birth:

"After this Job opened his mouth and cursed the day of his birth. And Job spoke and said: 'May the day perish on which I was born, And the night in which it was said, 'A male child is conceived.' May that day be darkness; May God above not seek it, Nor the light shine upon it. May darkness and the shadow of death claim it; May a cloud settle on it; May the blackness of the day terrify it. As for that night, may darkness seize it; May it not rejoice among the days of the year, May it not come into the number of the months. Oh, may that night be barren! May no joyful shout come into it! May those curse it who curse the day, Those who are ready to arouse Leviathan. May the stars of its morning be dark; May it look for light, but have none, And not seen the dawning of the day; Because it did not shut up the doors of my mother's womb, Nor hide sorrow from my eyes. Why did I not die at birth? Why did I not perish when I came from the womb? Why did the knees receive me? Or why the breasts, that I should nurse? For now I would have lain still and been quiet, I would have been asleep; Then I would have been at rest With kings and counsellors of the earth, Who built ruins for themselves, Or with princes who had gold, Who filled their houses with silver; Or why was I not hidden like a stillborn child, Like infants who never saw light?''' (Job 1:3-6, NKJV).

But there is consolation for all that Job went through:

"Now the Lord blessed the latter days of Job more than his beginning; for he had fourteen thousand sheep, six thousand camels, one thousand yoke of oxen, and one thousand female donkeys." (Job 42:12, NKJV)

This confirms another scripture:

"For His anger is but for a moment, His favour is for life; Weeping may endure for a night, but joy comes in the morning." (Psalm 30:5, NKJV).

I have realised that everything in life is an option:

- Suicide is an option
- Giving up is an option
- Depression is an option
- Running away is also an option

But hope is the key to avoiding these negative options. Keep hope alive, and trust in God's timing and blessings.

Rolling the Dice

On the table, I watched as you rolled the dice
Triple sixes, one after another
A streak of fortune that left me in awe
The dice seemed to favour you
Rewarding every toss with the highest marks
Inspired by your success, I tried my hand
But each roll brought me numbers lower than the last
What startled me most was the final throw
When the dice rolled and revealed a two
Why me? I wondered, why this difference?
We put in the same efforts, yet our outcomes diverge
And I've heard it said that effort should yield the same result
But here, the same dice, the same table, the same effort,
Delivered different fates, different scores
Is it true, then, that life is not always fair?
That all fingers are not equal
Some longer, some shorter?
A force that whispers, favour is better than labour.
When you trek and I drive
We may both reach the destination
But at different times, under different skies

So, I choose to let go of envy

To make peace with your achievements

And focus on my own journey

For what good comes from burdening myself with your success?

My load is heavy enough

My path challenging enough

I need no further weight on my shoulders

I will keep rolling the dice

And I will keep celebrating my scores

For perhaps a time will come

When it will be my season

For high scores and winning rolls

Rolling the Dice

Have you ever wondered why it's always you, like the famous footballer Balotelli "why is it always me"? I have asked this particular question many times over when life seems to be battle always. I have tried my hands on many projects many ventures and it look as if I may have to keep trying and it look as if there is no limit to the many times I have to try.

Life seems so many times unfair especially when you watch your others succeed with ease in many areas you have had to continually struggle. In my years as a student, I have many times question the fact that we are all students under the same teacher especially for me subjects like of Mathematics seems to be a very difficult and impossible challenge to me and in the same class there are students who feels so comfortable and at home with all the challenges thrown at them. It's an irony a difficult narrative that I struggle to understand.

It's not all a gloom as I always rejoice when it's lesson time for Literature, Economics, and such subjects that does not need much of calculations. So, it can be true that one man's food is another man's poison.

Every week I see a lot of many people play all forms of bets with so many promises and expectations of large winning bonuses, but the most interesting thing is that only few people can boast of ever winning big, but this has. not deter many millions of people trying their luck weeks after weeks and it can be so annoying when you hear of stories of people who just tried for the first time and win effortlessly what has become an albatross challenge to everybody.

This has just gone to prove King Solomon right in the book of Ecclesiastical that time and chance happens to them all. Another interesting quote is that the race is not for the swift neither is the battle for the strong.

Looking at the way that Prophet Elijah prayed for the rain on Mount Carmel,

"Then Elijah said to Ahab, "Go up, eat and drink; for there is the sound of abundance of rain." So, Ahab went up to eat and drink. And Elijah went up to the top of Carmel; then he bowed down on the ground, and put his face between his knees, and said to his servant, "Go up now, look toward the sea." So, he went up and looked, and said, "There is nothing." And seven times he said, "Go again." Then it came to pass the seventh time, that he said, "There is a cloud, as small as a man's hand, rising out of the sea!" So, he said, "Go up, say to Ahab, 'Prepare your chariot, and go down before the rain stops you.'" Now it happened in the meantime that the sky became black with clouds and wind, and there was a heavy rain. So, Ahab rode away and went to Jezreel." 1 Kings 18:41-45 (NKJV).

This was a great encounter that reveals the doggedness and conviction of the Prophet, he was not discouraged or contemplated on the idea of giving up he kept sending his servant to check for the signs of the impending rain even when it does not look as if something was about to happen. As a result, the cloud began to gather and eventually it was a mighty outpouring of rain.

Even if I have failed before, it's not considered as final until I stopped to try and like someone said you are not a failure until you give up on trying.

I love boxing as you would notice that to declare you a Champion you have to go for 12 rounds and if you have been doing very well from round one to round 11 as long as your opponent is still standing there is hope because if he manages to land a Knockout in round 12 all your efforts from the other rounds is of no consequence, so please don't quit as quitters don't win and winners don't quit.

There could not have been any better way than the way King Solomon also put it when he said God makes all things beautiful in his time, which is very deep as nobody seems to know when the time is ripe.

The best way and mostly rewarding is to rejoice with those that rejoice as it becomes a seed you are sowing towards your own harvest; this is what the holy book encourages us to do is of no use wishing people evil or feeling unnecessarily jealous of their achievements or accomplishments knowing fully well that your days of rejoicing is just across the corner.

I pray that all of labours are handsomely rewarded as I have been there many times, and most times it always come through, imagine as a Pastor you are the one that prays for Couples who are trying for a child and people testifies that God do answer when you pray and suddenly, you now find yourself having to pray for the same prayer points you have prayed for others. My wife and myself had to wait for seven years for our first child, and I have a friend who had to wait for sixteen years but guessed what it finally happened for us all. In case you are in our situation presently I have good news and a strong conviction that thou it tarries it will come to pass.

I Am Not Guilty

I am Not Guilty

I wish you could see what I saw

I am not guilty

Hope the jury can say unanimously

Discharged and acquitted

Come inside

Leaning on the railing won't produce the answer

Be bold, take time

Look beyond the outside

Packaging sometimes fails to celebrate the content

The first glance won't suffice

Give it another trial

Action does not always justify reaction

I am black, but white

Sometimes grey, depending on your view

I wish I could muster a better explanation

But words fail to give the right answer

Seeing the consequential mess

As part of the jury, I understand your struggle

It takes effort and courage to hear the inner voice

Saying the conviction is not right

The top of the mountain is the place to see

The beauty of the valley

However, it takes strength to reach the tip

So don't give up

Keep pushing, keep trying, keep shining

Keep going – in other words, keep on keeping up

To reach the sky

You must rise above the horizon

Right now, I am too old to start over

And too young to quit

I sometimes wish it could return

To the state at birth, when all was tabula rasa

Whichever way, at whatever level

All I see is hope

I am not guilty

Do you have an idea of how many People are victim of stigmatisation?

They are tired of how many times they have to explain themselves, sometimes not necessarily down to what they have done. This word is so unfair many people are just tired, but no matter how they tried they are considered guilty. The way the world system operates can be so judgemental and unfriendly.

I remember vividly in one of my many messages that I encouraged my Church members to love their neighbours as themselves according to the biblical injunction, I hardly finished preaching that someone approached me to say so what happened when you don't even love yourself so how do I love someone else. Many people are victims of circumstances they find themselves and greatly misunderstood.

It can be so bad even to struggle with who you are.

I remember people call you different names stereotyping people based on their looks and the many challenges they are faced with.

My parents should have been accused on my height, my looks and many of my physical disabilities as all these external features is a result of the gene that I carried, unfortunately I was not preview to my parents' marriage and also when they decided to have children they did not even seek for my permission, so what you see in me today is the consequences I faced based on other people's decisions therefore to accuse me of being guilty is unfair.

There are so many things that happen in our lives, that has nothing to do with our own contributions then we can gladly convince ourselves even if it is practically impossible to convince other people of our sincere innocence.

How strong are you to not base your judgement on what you see, what they say most especially when what you are being told makes sense appealing to your five senses.

In philosophy we were taught about the concept of ethics and there are two major concepts in moral ethics that calls for our attention these are concept of relativism and absolutism there are some concepts that is considered relative, which means that the right or wrong of a situation is dependent upon the people, time, place, culture and range of other factors so to pass absolute judgement on so many issues may not be expedient. Your skin, your tribe, your story has made some people pass, judgement on your character your predicament and your challenges.

What will you do when you find out that you have mistakenly judge someone or you have attributed or contributed ignorantly to somebody's pain.

There is a lot that happens around us every day and in hindsight when you have access to more information You may now notice that your conclusion must have been a bit rash call and unjustified.

I am learning not to judge people until I have all the information that is required to make an intelligent decision on matters of importance. People go through different tasking situations. Imagine when you hear of couples getting a divorce. I think the best approach is to avoid condemning them take time to listen to their stories and then see how you can be of help instead of judging them.

The best approach is to avoid condemning people imagine when Jesus looked into the eyes of the woman caught in adultery John 8:3-11.

"Then the scribes and Pharisees brought to Him a woman caught in adultery. And when they had set her in the midst, they said to Him, "Teacher, this woman was caught in adultery, in the very act. Now Moses, in the law, commanded us that such should be stoned. But what do You say?" This they said, testing Him, that they might have something of which to accuse Him. But Jesus stooped down and wrote on the ground with His finger, as though He did not hear. So, when they continued asking Him, He raised Himself up and said to them, "He who is without sin among you, let him throw a stone at her first." And again, He stooped down and wrote on the ground. Then those who heard it, being convicted by their conscience, went out one by one, beginning with the oldest even to the last. And Jesus was left alone, and the woman standing in the midst. When Jesus had raised Himself up and saw no one but the woman, He said to her, "Woman, where are those accusers of yours? Has no one condemned you?" She said, "No one, Lord." And Jesus said to her, "Neither do I condemn you; go and sin no more.""

The most powerful statement Jesus made was in verse 1" neither do I". I was also of the opinion that it is possible that Jesus was coming from an angle, or he had a better understanding of the woman's predicament, And I've noticed that one of the hallmarks of Jesus 's ministry was to restore hope to the hopeless and give opportunity for a new beginning for everyone that he had an encounter with.

If Jesus can stoop so low to engage a Samaritan woman at The Well in John chapter 4 versus 6 to 26 "Now Jacob's well was there. Jesus, therefore, being wearied from His journey, sat thus by the well. It was about the sixth hour. A woman of Samaria came to draw water. Jesus said to her, "Give Me a drink." For His disciples had gone away into the city to buy food. Then the woman of Samaria said to Him, "How is it that You, being a Jew, ask a drink from me, a Samaritan woman?" For Jews have no dealings with Samaritans. Jesus answered and said to her, "If you knew the gift of God, and who it is who says to you, 'Give Me a drink,' you would have asked Him, and He would have given you living water." The woman said to Him, "Sir, You have nothing to draw with, and the well is deep. Where then do You get that living water? Are You greater than our father Jacob, who gave us the well, and drank from it himself, as well as his sons and his livestock?" Jesus answered and said to her, "Whoever drinks of this water will thirst again, but whoever drinks of the water that I shall give him will never thirst. But the water that I shall give him will become in him a fountain of water springing up into everlasting life." The woman said to Him, "Sir, give me this water, that I may not thirst, nor come here to draw." Jesus said to her, "Go, call your husband, and come here." The woman answered and said, "I have no husband." Jesus said to her, "You have well said, 'I have no husband,' for you have had five husbands, and the one whom you now have is not your husband; in that you spoke truly." The woman said to Him, "Sir, I perceive that You are a prophet. Our fathers worshiped on this mountain, and you Jews say that in Jerusalem is the place where one ought to worship." Jesus said to her, "Woman, believe Me, the hour is coming when you will neither on this mountain, nor in Jerusalem, worship the Father. You worship what you do not know; we know what we worship, for salvation is of the Jews. But the hour is coming, and now is, when the true worshipers will worship the Father in spirit and truth; for the Father is seeking such to worship Him. God is Spirit, and those who worship Him must worship in spirit and truth." The woman said to Him, "I know that Messiah is coming" (who is called Christ). "When He comes, He will tell us all things." Jesus said to her, "I who speak to you am He.""

Despite the past of this woman in fact the disciples were so shocked to see such a holy man engaging such a sinner and this was evidence in their response in verse 27. Many failed marriages, knowing the experiences of this woman with men Jesus was still accessible to her. What a saviour?

Like someone said truth is dynamic and relative some things which are facts now after some more evidence become untenable and unfounded.

There is one story in the Bible that completely drives home this whole story of wrong accusation and betrayal. The story of Joseph and Potiphar's wife. Genesis 39:6-20.

"Thus, he left all that he had in Joseph's hand, and he did not know what he had except for the bread which he ate. Now Joseph was handsome in form and appearance. And it came to pass after these things that his master's wife cast longing eyes on Joseph, and she said, "Lie with me." But he refused and said to his master's wife, "Look, my master does not know what is with me in the house, and he has committed all that he has to my hand. There is no one greater in this house than I, nor has he kept back anything from me but you, because you are his wife. How then can I do this great wickedness, and sin against God?" So it was, as she spoke to Joseph, day by day, that he did not heed her, to lie with her or to be with her. But it happened about this time, when Joseph went into the house to do his work, and none of the men of the house was inside, that she caught him by his garment, saying, "Lie with me." But he left his garment in her hand, and ed and ran outside. And so it was, when she saw that he had left his garment in her hand and ran outside, that she called to the men of her house and spoke to them, saying, "See, he has brought in to us a Hebrew to mock us. He came in to me to lie with me, and I cried out with a loud voice. And it happened, when he heard that I lifted my voice and cried out, that he left his garment with me, and ed and went outside." So, she kept his garment with her until his master came home. Then she spoke to him with words like these, saying, "The Hebrew servant whom you brought to us came in to me to mock me; so, it happened, as I lifted my voice and cried out, that he left his garment with me and ed outside." So it was, when his master heard the words which his wife spoke to him, saying, "Your servant did to me after this manner," that his anger was aroused. Then Joseph's master took him and put him into the prison, a place where the king's prisoners were kept. And he was there in the prison".

Up till tomorrow, the greatest regret of Joseph was that he left his garment in the hand of this deceptive woman and this woman used that garment to our utmost advantage how do you argue or defend yourself with such overwhelming evidence.

Despite the fact that the Egyptian master had a lot of regard for the poor boy Joseph, but the garment of Joseph in the hand of this woman had made the judgement very difficult for, everybody.

There was such an incident in my life some years back, I was working for a friend and this friend promised to give me a certain percentage as my wages from the total profit that we made. But to my greatest surprise this guy each time I worked for him he would tell me to wait for my payment and this was the trend of his behaviour promise upon promise to pay me after the next project.

And I was so trusting I thought he was sincere and honest. As time goes by it was becoming embarrassing for him not to pay so one day after we finished one of our projects we were lodged in a hotel and in the middle of the night while I was fast asleep, he woke me up and asked me to go to the trunk of his car, to bring for him an umbrella. I still did not put any meaning to his action because I should have wondered what would be the need for an umbrella in the middle of the night when there was no sign of rain but I obeyed him and when I checked the trunk of the car, obviously there was nothing like an umbrella so I returned to him and explained that there was nothing like that at the trunk of the car, he did not argue with me. He told me that I can go back to sleep. The next morning, he gave me an excuse that the hotel environment was not conducive to share money, but I should return to his house in two weeks' time when my payment will have been made ready. I trusted him and I left for my house which was in a different city waiting for the two weeks as agreed. I cannot wait for the appointment with excitement, I went back to my friend house for my payment as at that time I was in rent areas and all my mind was that my predicament was about to come to an end.

On this faithful as I enter my friend's house, I met him and one of his other friends sitting in his balcony, and as I greeted him warmly, he was so cold, and I was taking aback as I was wondering what could've gone wrong. My so-called friend then look into his other friends' eyes and said that is the man 'the pastor' he was talking about. I was still very confused on the development when his friend now said to me, but pastor why? I questioned him what exactly are you talking about and he said that he was informed by my so-called friend that the night he woke me up to collect the umbrella from his car trunk he later noticed that I must've stolen some of his money because all the taking for the business was kept at the back of the car, so I must have helped myself to his money. I was so lost, confused, and disappointed and surprised, my legs started to shake. I tried to cry, but tears refused to flow. The guy can tell that I was completely shocked and before I could utter any word in my defence my friend threatened to invite the police if I do not quickly find my way out of his compound. The other friend that was him did not even give me any chance to defend myself, I felt humiliated and defeated. It was so bad that I do not even have enough money for my transportation back to my city, so you can imagine how humiliating this experience was for me. When I left this compound confused, I did remember that close to his house was another friend's house, so I had to trek to that my friend's house. Fortunately, he was at home as I entered his house, and he asked me what the matter looking at my countenance. I just busted into tears. I could not even explain what I just witnessed, the guy allowed me to cry for as long as I wanted and when I stopped crying, I narrated the whole ordeal to him but surprisingly he was not too surprised, and he said that what I just witnessed was nothing but a game they just played on me. The guy knew I was not guilty, but the problem is now how many people hearing the story from my dubious friend that will believe my own version of the story. Up unto this moment I still sometimes feel the pain and looking back I sometimes laughed and wonder how naive I have been.

There are a lot of people behind bars, and in all sincerity, they are victims of consequential evidence that is impossible to defend or to plead their innocence, to such people I dedicate this poem. Sometimes words are not good enough to express your heart. I have learnt that journey of life can sometimes be lonely complicated and very difficult to navigate. Not every story have a happy ending like that of Joseph who became Prime Minister despite all the ordeals of going through prison and been accused wrongly, it was bad enough to be sold as a slave by your blood brothers and now to face another conspiracy of lies and wrong accusation can be very devastating and challenging, learning from Joseph example I have come to realise that it is not advisable to lose faith in difficult.

Worksheet for Reflection

1. Pray for Those Wrongfully Imprisoned or Condemned
    - Action Step:
        - o Dedicate time each day to pray for individuals who have been wrongfully imprisoned or condemned.
    - Prayer Points:
        - o Pray for their strength and resilience during their ordeal.
        - o Ask for justice to prevail and for their wrongful convictions to be overturned. • Seek comfort and peace for their families and loved ones.
    - Sample Prayer:

"Dear Lord, we lift up those who have been wrongfully imprisoned or condemned. Grant them strength and courage as they endure this unjust situation. May truth and justice prevail, leading to their freedom. Comfort their families and loved ones during this difficult time. Amen."

2. Reflect on Your Own Judgments
    - Action Step:
        - o Take time to introspect and identify moments where you have been judgmental.

- Reflection Questions:
    - When have I judged others without knowing their full story?
    - How can I cultivate more empathy and understanding in my interactions?
    - What steps can I take to be less judgmental in the future?
- Commitment Statement:
    - "I commit to being more empathetic and less judgmental in my daily life. I will strive to understand others' perspectives and withhold judgment until I have all the facts."

3. Reach Out to Friends or Family Members
    - Action Step:
        - Contact friends or family members you haven't heard from recently to offer your support.
    - Methods of Contact:
        - Call or text them to check in and express your care.
        - Send a thoughtful card or letter to let them know you're thinking of them.
        - Plan a visit or virtual meet-up to reconnect and catch up.

- Sample Message:

"Hi [Friend/Family Member's Name],

I've been thinking about you and wanted to check in. How have you been? I'm here for you if you need anything or just want to talk. Let's catch up soon! Take care,

[Your Name]"

- Reflection Exercise:
    - Journal Prompt: Write about a time when you felt judged or misunderstood. How did it impact you? What could others have done differently to be more supportive?
    - Gratitude List: Create a list of people who have shown you understanding and support. Reflect on how their empathy made a difference in your life.
- Additional Tips:
    - Set Reminders: Schedule regular reminders to pray, reflect, and reach out to loved ones.
    - Create a Support System: Form a group with friends or community members to share these reflections and support each other in these actions.

Stay Consistent: Make these activities a regular part of your routine to cultivate a more empathetic and supportive lifestyle.

The King's Silence

The king entered his closet, the door shut tight
Few expected him to come for a dance
After what seemed like endless waiting
One by one, they left, disheartened
The market square grew empty, neglected, and quiet
For how long, they asked?
What can we do, they wondered?
In their frustration, they consulted the oracle
Hoping for a glimpse of good news
But alas, it brought no promise
Even the oracle seemed cautious
Afraid of being quoted out of context
Thus, Shh became the song of the square
Yet from nowhere, a noise gathered momentum
Growing more convincing with each echo
Birds flew towards the sound
Surprised, they added their voices
A new horizon began to make sense
But still, they questioned
Would it be another fleeting sound?
As doubts rose, the sound grew intense
Dogs barked, tails wagging with excitement

Unexpected, to say the least

Let us dance, let us celebrate

The wine is restored, tasting better than before

Perhaps there is a new wine tapper in town

Dance, dance, they cried

Drink, drink, they echoed

Flow, flourish, and be fruitful

This is the dawn of a new day

A new beginning

Never worry, it has come to stay

That is the news in the city

The King's Silence

There are times in life when words fail to capture the essence of what we are going through. In such moments, silence becomes a powerful ally. It's not that we lack the words to express ourselves, but rather that words would be superfluous and ineffective. Silence allows us to weigh our thoughts and emotions, offering clarity in the midst of chaos.

Many people misunderstand silence, feeling offended or disappointed by it. Yet, as the saying goes, "silence is golden." It can provide space for introspection and peace, offering wisdom that words cannot convey.

Even our best predictions can fail, and it's wise to approach the future with humility and openness. By doing so, we prepare ourselves to embrace the unexpected without confusion or fear. Change is inevitable, and with it comes the opportunity for transformation. Miracles often occur when we least expect them, reminding us that hope is never in vain.

Consider the wedding at Cana of Galilee, a story that perfectly illustrates the unexpected nature of miracles:

"And when they ran out of wine, the mother of Jesus said to Him, 'They have no wine.'" John 2:3 (NKJV).

In the midst of a joyful celebration, the wine suddenly ran out – an unforeseen crisis that threatened to cast a shadow over the festivities. The bride and groom, likely overwhelmed and embarrassed, faced a potential social disaster. Yet, in this moment of crisis, Jesus intervened, transforming the situation from one of despair to one of triumph by turning water into wine.

"When the master of the feast had tasted the water that was made wine, and did not know where it came from (but the servants who had drawn the water knew), the master of the feast called the bridegroom. And he said to him, 'Every man at the beginning sets out the good wine, and when the guests have well drunk, then the inferior. You have kept the good wine until now!'" John 2:9-10 (NKJV).

The master of the feast, unaware of the miracle that had taken place, praised the bride and groom for saving the best wine for last. What began as a potential embarrassment was transformed into a moment of honour and joy.

This story teaches us that even in our darkest moments, a divine turnaround is possible. Do not become so accustomed to problems that you hesitate to celebrate your successes. Embrace joy and trust that your celebrations will endure, even when they come unexpectedly or after a long period of waiting.

Get used to celebrating your achievements and savouring the joy that comes with them. Let go of unnecessary doubts about the possibility of failure and embrace the belief that good things are on the horizon.

Your fortune will be restored, and everything taken from you will return in abundance. Friends who have distanced themselves will come back to celebrate with you. This is your rightful inheritance, and it is what you can expect as you move forward with faith and optimism.

Self-Reflection and Personal Growth Worksheet

This worksheet aims to help you appreciate your personal strengths, understand the power of silence, embrace positivity, and manage fears. By working through these exercises, you will develop a deeper sense of self-awareness and resilience.

1. Appreciate Your Strength of Character

Objective: Recognise and celebrate your inner strengths and qualities.

Task: Reflect on your personal qualities that have helped you navigate life's challenges.

- Identify Your Strengths:
  - List at least three qualities or strengths you possess (e.g., resilience, empathy, perseverance).
  - Think of specific situations where these strengths helped you overcome challenges.
- Reflect on Growth:
  - Consider how these strengths have evolved over time.
  - Acknowledge any new skills or qualities you have developed recently.

- Celebrate Your Achievements:
    - Write a brief statement celebrating your character and achievements.

Example: "I am proud of my resilience and ability to adapt to change. These qualities have helped me overcome obstacles and continue to grow."

2. Celebrate the Power of Silence

Objective: Recognise the value of silence in handling difficult situations.

Task: Reflect on how silence has been beneficial in your life.

- Reflect on Past Experiences:
    - Think of times when choosing silence over words helped you navigate a situation.
    - Consider how silence allowed you to listen, reflect, and gain clarity.
- Evaluate the Impact:
    - Assess how these moments of silence contributed to personal growth or resolution.
    - Write down why these experiences were valuable to you.
- Celebrate Your Wisdom:
    - Acknowledge your ability to choose silence wisely.

Example: "By embracing silence, I have learned to listen and understand more deeply, allowing for thoughtful responses and personal peace."

3. Embrace Positivity

Objective: Cultivate a positive mindset and understand its importance in your life.

Task: Convince yourself of the benefits of maintaining a positive attitude.

- Identify Positive Influences:
    - List activities, people, or environments that inspire positivity in your life.
    - Reflect on how these influences improve your mood and outlook.
- Understand the Benefits:
    - Write down the advantages of being positive, such as increased happiness, improved relationships, and better health.
- Practice Positivity:
    - Commit to one positive habit you will incorporate into your daily routine (e.g., gratitude journaling, daily affirmations).

Example Affirmation: "I choose to see the good in every situation and believe that positivity will guide me through challenges."

4. Manage Your Fears

Objective: Acknowledge and address your fears constructively.

Task: Understand that not all fears become reality and learn to manage them effectively.

- Identify Your Fears:
    - List some common fears or anxieties you experience.
    - Consider how they affect your thoughts and actions.
- Evaluate the Likelihood:
    - Reflect on past fears that never materialised and what you learned from those experiences.
    - Write down why some fears may be exaggerated or unfounded.
- Develop Coping Strategies:
    - Identify methods to manage your fears, such as deep breathing, visualization, or talking to a trusted friend.
- Affirmation for Overcoming Fear:

"Not all fears will come true, and I am equipped to handle any challenges that arise with courage and resilience."

5. Final Reflection:

After completing these exercises, take a moment to reflect on your insights and growth. Consider how you can integrate these practices into your daily life to foster ongoing personal development and resilience.

The New Dance

I wish I could explain better as we all share this confusion
I checked the script; it seems totally unscripted and unexpected
Have you heard? The Masquerade can no longer hold the night dance. It's in the open now, and the rhythm is no longer the same
The Masquerade dances Azonto, meant only for the elders in the forest
But the steps do not align with the percussion
The announcement is unclear; something has melded up along the line. Can we maintain a straight path? I ask, but no one seems to care. The flowing gown, too colourful in my judgment
Is not the designer's fault; everyone added their own hue
Now it's a riot of colours but lacks any pattern
The sage wonders how long this can go on
Will the drum not burst? It's overworked already
Not designed to be beaten for this long
My predictions were wrong
I told my neighbour the sound would soon quiet, and we'd soon be snoring
But the sound grew louder, even in the distant woods

Ask the foxes what they are doing in the open, in the heart of downtown

Their response was daring: to open an office for their representation, as they could trust no one in the city council

I wait and will write a poem when this finally ends,

And the city can finally sleep

The New Dance

In today's world, confusion reigns. Traditional norms and roles have shifted dramatically, leaving many uncertain about what is acceptable. Relationships that were once controversial, like Adam marrying Steve, are now met with indifference. Just a few years ago, gender roles were more clearly defined, but now everything seems ambiguous and disordered.

In philosophy, we learn that a philosophical question cannot be answered with certainty. Every idea matter, and any question with a specific, accurate answer ceases to be philosophical. Our present world resembles a philosophical conundrum, with no absolute truths and ever-shifting norms.

Ethics appear to be relative, with no absolute morals guiding us. If our ancestors could see us now, they would be shocked at how much has changed. The biblical tale of Sodom and Gomorrah, as described in Genesis 18:20 (NKJV),

"And the Lord said, "Because the outcry against Sodom and Gomorrah is great, and because their sin is very grave,"

And in Genesis 19:4-5 (NKJV),

"Now before they lay down, the men of the city, the men of Sodom, both old and young, all the people from every quarter, surrounded the house. And they called to Lot and said to him, "Where are the men who came to you tonight? Bring them out to us that we may know them carnally."

Men of Sodom want to know the Men visiting carnally? What a shame? This serves as a stark reminder of past transgressions. Yet, our current actions far surpass those of Sodom and Gomorrah.

How long can we sustain this direction? Morally, we seem bankrupt, and worse, people appear apathetic. We have lost our sense of responsibility and dignity. There are no limits, no checks and balances. What one person considers good cannot be condemned by another. It's reminiscent of Romans 1:28-32, where people are described as having debased minds, filled with all kinds of unrighteousness.

Brotherly kindness is rare, and trust within families is fragile. The question on everyone's mind is: Where are we heading? If Generation Z is like this, what will happen to the next generation? We thought we had seen it all with the millennial generation, but the future seems even more alarming.

Technological advancements and social media have turned the world into a global village. You can be involved in anything without being physically present. The pace of change is rapid and relentless, widening the gap between generations. Issues like polygamy and open relationships challenge traditional notions of marriage. Such practices are becoming normalized, and few see anything wrong with them.

Even marijuana is legally promoted in places like Canada, without much concern for its consequences. These are just a few examples of the challenges facing my generation. If we don't act soon, as someone once said, we are drawing closer to the end each day. This trend is not limited to the secular world; even the church is in crisis. Doctrinal beliefs are being challenged, and efforts are made to redefine biblical injunctions to suit contemporary issues. Can we truly say that salvation is exclusive to Christianity in this age of ecumenism? The church needs another defining statement of faith, like the Nicene Creed, which was created to unify Christian beliefs. However, it would be much harder to achieve today, given our dynamic and ever-changing world. The best attitude is to expect the unexpected because, if we pretend not to be concerned, we are deluding ourselves. this rate, anything is possible.

Daily Watchlist (Prayer Focus)

1. Pray for Your Children
   - Intention: Ask for protection and clarity for your children amidst any confusion.
   - Prayer: "Lord, please safeguard my children from confusion and guide them with Your wisdom and clarity."
2. Pray for Countries in Conflict
   - Intention: Seek peace and resolution for countries experiencing war.

- Prayer: "Heavenly Father, bring peace to all nations at war. Comfort those affected and guide them towards reconciliation."

3. Pray for Politicians and Policy Makers
   - Intention: Request divine guidance for those in positions of power and influence.
   - Prayer: "God, guide our politicians and policy makers as they create policies that affect our lives. Grant them wisdom and compassion."

Reflection Questions

1. How can I support my children through times of confusion and ensure their wellbeing?
2. What are some specific countries currently in conflict that I can pray for?
3. How can I stay informed about policies and support good governance in my community?
4. What actions can I take to contribute to peace and positive change in my surroundings?

No Freeze In Breeze

I love the free style, celebrating freedom in style
Surfing waves in the middle of nowhere; guards down, brakes off, wild and free
The pot covered, steam struggles to find rhythm, to express.
Open the lid, remove the limits, feet off the pedal, let us have a blast
Adventurous, daunting as it looks, there's joy in the beauty of expression.
Why gauge me?
You showed me there's more to explore, so why the limits, rules, and worries?
Afraid I may fall, fail, and bruise?
If I do, it's part of the beautiful story
The scars will tell of battles fought, of courage that didn't bow to fear
The bird sings even when caged, but never wished for the cage.
Let it out today, and your fear might end
You taught me to speak, so why cover my lips?
Let me speak, let me yearn, for I'm ready to burst

Last time you unblocked the dam, see the damage it caused

Why?

Because the water stayed too long without expression

Its anger real when finally released

When I love, I love freely

When I care, with passion

Until there's no tomorrow, my love will always be free

Stay strong, maintain your lane

This isn't Glasgow where roads are made of glass

It looks fragile, but it won't break

It's just the design

There is strength in freedom

There is no freeze in breeze

No Freeze In Breeze

When you find freedom, you find peace – they are twins. You cannot find one without the other. We live in a world filled with fear, where the freedom to express ourselves is often accompanied by the constant worry of being misunderstood. This anxiety puts a significant strain on our lives, making us perpetually cautious.

My parents tried their best to guide me through life. They sought to protect me from many things with good intentions. However, I have realised that some of these protections were unnecessary, as it is often better to learn from one's own mistakes. Failure, both internal and external, helps us fully appreciate success.

One of the greatest lessons from the Bible is the story of the Prodigal Son (Luke 15:11-24): "A certain man had two sons. The younger said to his father, 'Father, give me my share of the estate.' So, he divided his property between them. Not long after, the younger son got together all he had, set off for a distant country, and squandered his wealth in wild living. After he had spent everything, there was a severe famine, and he began to be in need. So, he went and hired himself out to a citizen of that country, who sent him to his fields to feed pigs. He longed to fill his stomach with the pods the pigs were eating, but no one gave him anything. When he came to his senses, he said, 'How many of my father's hired servants have food to spare, and here I am starving to death! I will set out and go back to my father and say to him: Father, I have sinned against heaven and against you. I am no longer worthy to be called your son; make me like one of your hired servants.' So, he got up and went to his father. But while he was still a long way off, his father saw him and was filled with compassion; he ran to his son, threw his arms around him, and kissed him. The son said to him, 'Father, I have sinned against heaven and against you. I am no longer worthy to be called your son.' But the father said to his servants, 'Quick! Bring the best robe and put it on him. Put a ring on his finger and sandals on his feet. Bring the fattened calf and kill it. Let's have a feast and celebrate. For this son of mine was dead and is alive again; he was lost and is found.' So, they began to celebrate." I have often wondered how a father with only two children could be so caring and protective yet allow one of them to walk away. He knew his son couldn't survive on his own, but trying to convince him otherwise would have been futile, and the boy might have resented his father for life. The boy would have blamed his father for not believing in him.

Instead of sending out a search party or looking for the young man himself, the father stood his ground, likely praying for his son's safety without knowing his whereabouts. How many fathers today can do what this man did? Interestingly, the story does not mention the mother. Whether deliberate or due to divorce, it focuses on the father's actions:

1. He gave the boy his portion when asked.
2. He did not question the young man's intentions.
3. He did not send out a search party.
4. He allowed the boy to follow his plan, despite knowing he would struggle.

The story implies the family might never see the boy again, as he left in a hurry without a concrete plan. Each passing day likely brought disappointment until the boy decided to return. Someone once said he left as a boy but returned as a man, having learned from his experiences.

The father's forgiveness showed he recognised his son had finally matured.

In my experience, I once had a son who was stubborn and determined to chart his own path. Despite my counsel, he did what he thought was best until he found himself in jail. During a prison visit, I asked why he had ignored my advice. He said he believed he was invincible. Prison made him realise his mistakes, leading to his transformation. Must it always take such extreme circumstances for change?

My father in the Lord shared an experience with his son in Amsterdam. Despite his advice not to drink from a stream, his son did, thinking his father's caution was due to being from Africa. Later, the boy suffered severe stomach-ache, learning a hard lesson about heeding advice. In Deuteronomy 8:2-3,

"And you shall remember that the Lord your God led you all the way these forty years in the wilderness, to humble you and test you, to know what was in your heart, whether you would keep His commandments or not. So, He humbled you, allowed you to hunger, and fed you with manna which you did not know nor did your fathers know, that He might make you know that man shall not live by bread alone; but man lives by every word that proceeds from the mouth of the Lord."

God allowed Israel to experience hunger to humble them, showing that He trains His children by exposing them to different sides of life. If God does this, why do we shield our children from life's realities?

In England, eye contact and a firm handshake are signs of respect, contrary to what I learned growing up in Africa. This cultural difference once caused a judge to misinterpret my respect as insincerity, highlighting how lack of exposure can be a significant disadvantage. In our present world the struggle to be oneself is real. Don't try to be like anyone else; enjoy being yourself. Many are influenced by friends, society, and other factors, ending up living to please others. My philosophy is that life is for living – enjoy every moment, and don't live with regrets. I encourage trying new things without fear of failure. Failure is not the end but a teacher. Those who try and fail gain more experience than those who never try, thus never being considered true failures. Let us determine to live fully, not just exist, for life is for the giving.

Daily Watchlist

Gratitude

- Thank God for all the positive and negative experiences of the past.
- Reflect on both the blessings and the challenges, recognizing how they have shaped you. Affirmation

Affirm yourself with scripture

"And we know that all things work together for good to those who love God, to those who are called according to His purpose" (Romans 8:28).

Acts of Kindness

- Try to do something good or show unusual kindness to someone today. Think of a specific person or group you can help and plan an act of kindness.

Reflection Questions

1. What positive experiences from the past am I grateful for today?
2. How have the challenges I faced shaped me into who I am now?
3. In what ways can I remind myself that all things work together for good? 4. Who can I show kindness to today, and what specific action can I take? Notes

Use this space to jot down any thoughts, experiences, or insights you gain throughout the day.

When Can I Finally Say, "It Is Well?"

When can I finally say, "it is well"?
For when I overcome one mountain, trying to catch my breath
I realise it's time for another challenge
I can barely feel my hands, ready to take a nap
Then comes the whistle, signalling the start of another expedition.
Can you see the beautiful rainbow?
But how long will the sky remain this serene?
A question lingers at the back of my mind
Perhaps it's not time to ask, for your answer might insult my intelligence
But here is the issue: who can I trust not to wound my heart?
Good words do not necessarily mean a good heart
So, it's not your kind words that I need right now, but a kind heart. Even if your words are harsh, as long as your heart is true
They will be like the pain of childbirth: intense, excruciating
Yet when the baby survives the ordeal and the mother finally heals, the joy is deeply cherished

Let the oven be open, even though the aroma can be
torturous.
Rest, they say, is all I need, as if I don't know.
But how, when, and for how long? That is my greatest
worry.

When Can I say, "It Is Well?"

Bob Dylan, in his iconic song "Blowin' in the Wind," poignantly captures the essence of life's journey with the rhetorical question: "How many roads must a man walk down before you call him a man?" This question resonates deeply in today's complex and fast-paced world, where the struggle to keep up often feels overwhelming.

Life's challenges can feel insurmountable, and even the most resilient among us struggle to maintain balance. A critical question arises: how do we stay sane amid the chaos? Staying relevant and current in our modern world is a daunting task. Some argue that peace is preferable to happiness because happiness is often contingent on external factors, while peace is an internal state that persists despite life's challenges. To manage our lives effectively, we must find a balance that allows us to enjoy both peace and happiness.

Achieving this balance often requires significant sacrifices. These choices can be costly, as one cannot have it all. Even in the biblical account of creation, God found time to rest on the seventh day. While there are various interpretations of this rest, the simple understanding is crucial: rest is essential. Genesis 2:2-3 (NKJV) states: "And on the seventh day God ended His work which He had done, and He rested on the seventh day from all His work which He had done. Then God blessed the seventh day and sanctified it, because in it He rested from all His work which God had created and made." This passage underscores the non-negotiable nature of rest. Similarly, Exodus 20:8-11 (NKJV) emphasises the importance of the Sabbath: "Remember the Sabbath day, to keep it holy. Six days you shall labour and do all your work, but the seventh day is the Sabbath of the Lord your God. In it you shall do no work: you, nor your son, nor your daughter, nor your male servant, nor your female servant, nor your cattle, nor your stranger who is within your gates. For in six days the Lord made the heavens and the earth, the sea, and all that is in them, and rested the seventh day. Therefore, the Lord blessed the Sabbath day and hallowed it." Ignoring this commandment led to dire consequences for Israel, as they were exiled for seventy years due to their disregard for the Sabbath.

Disregarding the need for rest has significant repercussions. Our generation faces numerous challenges, partly due to our neglect of rest. Constant work without rest can lead to feelings of guilt when contemplating a break. However, if even the Creator rested, it is essential for us to follow this example. Violating this fundamental principle can lead to severe consequences. The rising rates of suicide and mental breakdowns are alarming, and the situation seems to be worsening. People are busier than ever, leading to increased stress and its associated health issues. The question remains: when will we make time for rest to prevent these unexpected breakdowns?

In the Western world, the relentless pace of life seems unsustainable, raising concerns about an impending crisis.

It is often said that we are sitting on a time bomb, as even the environment and our ecosystem are showing signs of stress. The debate over climate change cannot be ignored, as we witness unprecedented natural phenomena.

Stress affects everyone, contributing to various health issues, including cancer. Matthew 8:23-27 (NKJV) recounts how Jesus slept through a storm, demonstrating that rest is possible even amid turmoil. Similarly, in Acts 12:5-6 (NKJV), Peter slept peacefully in prison despite imminent danger, showing that faith can bring rest in dire circumstances.

We must find a way to escape the current insanity and create a safe haven for ourselves. As 1 Kings 20:40 (NKJV) warns, being perpetually busy can lead to dire consequences: "While your servant was busy here and there, he was gone." We need to break free from the syndrome of constant busyness.

In conclusion, while everyone talks about needing rest, we must move from words to action. Life should be viewed in terms of benefits and gains. When the benefits of rest outweigh the costs, it is wise to choose rest. Taking time to rejuvenate and refresh is essential for being physically and mentally refresh is essential so as b to maintain your well-being?

Worksheet and Reflection

Is it possible for you to find a destination for a holiday?

1. Dream Destination: Where would you like to go and why?
2. Planning Steps: What steps can you take to plan this holiday? (e.g., budgeting, researching destinations, booking accommodations)
3. Spiritual Retreat:
    - When was the last time you had a one-on-one retreat with God or engaged in spiritual reflection?
    - Describe the experience: How did it impact your spiritual life?
4. Future Plans: How can you incorporate regular spiritual retreats into your schedule?
5. Sleep Patterns:
    - What is your current sleep pattern?
    - Average Hours of Sleep: How many hours of sleep do you get per night?
    - Quality of Sleep: How restful is your sleep?
    - Do you wake up feeling refreshed?
    - Improvement Strategies: What changes can you make to improve your sleep quality? (e.g., establishing a bedtime routine, reducing screen time before bed)

6. Relaxation and Rejuvenation:
    - What activities or practices help you relax and rejuvenate?
    - List your top 5 relaxation activities: (e.g., reading, meditating, exercising)
    - Self-Care Routine: How can you incorporate these activities into your daily or weekly routine?

Benefits: How do these activities positively impact your mental and physical health?

7. Personal Action Plan:
    - Creating a Wellness Plan:
        - Short-Term Goals: What can you do this week to start improving your well-being?
        - Long-Term Goals: What are your wellness goals for the next six months?
    - Accountability: How will you hold yourself accountable to these goals? (e.g., tracking progress, enlisting a friend or coach for support.

A New Day

When morning breezes in with freshness, beauty, and calm
The world awakens in harmony
Birds sing, clocks chime, and the body stretches
Ready to embrace the dawn of a new day
For me, it is a profound joy to witness this renewal
A silent promise of hope
A reassurance that today may outshine the days gone by
As the Boy Scouts shout their motto, "Be Prepared,"
Their voices ring with a message clear and true
In their call, I find a deeper wisdom
While I rejoice in the birth of this day
I must also brace myself
For each day brings both light and shadow
This is the essence of life
A delicate balance of joy and sorrow
Some will greet the dawn with the cry of a newborn
A symbol of hope, a future unfolding
Others will face the day with tears
Mourning the loss of a loved one
Their hearts heavy with the weight of farewell
Some will step into new opportunities
Their path lit by fortune's favour

While others may stumble, losing what they've held dear
Their steps faltering on uncertain ground
This is the truth of a new day
A canvas painted in shades of ascent and descent
With each sunrise, life shifts and sways
Carrying us in two directions at once
So, I rejoice with hope
Mindful of the duality each day brings
And when sorrow touches my heart
I hold onto hope
Knowing that tomorrow may bring better tides
For every new day is a chance
A chance to rise, to fall
But always to begin anew

A New Day

Life is a journey woven with a complex tapestry of highs and lows, where every moment is fleeting and nothing is meant to last forever. Like the seasons, life is governed by cycles and timing.

Winter retreats as autumn ushers in the promise of spring, and spring bursts forth, heralding the warmth of summer. These cycles, seemingly repetitive, are what bring depth and beauty to our lives, each season leaving its indelible mark on the canvas of our existence.

When we close our eyes at night, we do so with the hope – not the certainty – of seeing another day. This hope is not a right, but a fragile privilege, one we often take for granted. Each dawn brings with it a blank page, a new chapter yet to be written, and with it, the promise of experiences unique to that day. However, not all days unfold as we expect. Some begin with joy and anticipation, only to be marred by unforeseen sorrow as the sun sets. Such is the nature of life – unpredictable and beyond our control. Yet, in the face of this uncertainty, we are called to live fully, embracing each moment without regret, for we do not know what the next hour might bring.

Jesus, in His wisdom, reminds us not to borrow trouble from tomorrow. "Sufficient for the day is its own evil," He says, urging us to focus on the present and not to add to the burdens that each day already carries. This divine counsel is a reminder that life is challenging enough without us heaping on additional worries.

I vividly remember the 23rd of December 2022 – a day that began with so much hope and ended in profound sorrow. My brother lay in a hospital bed, and I was filled with the expectation that he would recover, that he would soon be back on his feet. But as the day gave way to night, at the stroke of night, I received the call that shattered my world. My brother had gone to be with the Lord. I was alone in my car when the news came, and in that solitude, the tears flowed freely. I was thankful in that moment for the privacy of my grief, for the space to mourn without prying eyes. Yet, I also realized that vulnerability is not a sign of weakness. To cry, to feel deeply, is to be human. It is a testament to the love we carry in our hearts.

As a pastor, I have walked alongside many through their own valleys of despair, but one experience stands out vividly in my mind. On a particular Sunday morning, a dear member of our church, an elderly woman of grace and beauty, arrived late to the service. That day, I had decided to stand with the ushers, helping to gently remind latecomers of the importance of punctuality. I pulled her aside and spoke with her, reminding her that as a minister in our church, her example was important. She was deeply apologetic and assured me she would be more mindful in the future. After the service, she stopped by my office to apologize again, and we shared a laugh about the incident, parting ways with smiles.

The very next morning, my phone rang. It was a call I never expected. This same woman, who had been full of life and laughter just hours before, had been found unresponsive in her home and was being rushed to the hospital. I hurried to her side, but the doctors' words were grim. She had suffered an aneurysm, a silent and sudden rupture with little warning. Her chances of survival were slim, and within a week, she was gone. I found myself planning the funeral of a woman who had shown no signs of illness just days before. The fragility of life had never been more apparent.

Ministry is a constant balancing act between joy and sorrow, celebration and mourning. I recall one particular day when, after counselling a grieving couple who had just lost a pregnancy, my phone rang again. This time, it was a man on the other end, his voice filled with joy as he shared the news of a new job he had just secured after years of waiting and praying. In that moment, I was reminded of the duplicity of life – the way joy and sorrow coexist, often side by side. As a pastor, I have learned to navigate these extremes, to rejoice with those who rejoice and to weep with those who weep, sometimes within the span of a single day.

There was another instance that highlighted the delicate balance of trust and confidentiality in my role. A brother in our church approached me, seeking counsel as he prepared to propose to the woman he loved. He confided in me, asking for my advice and, importantly, my confidentiality, which I gladly offered. Shortly after, the woman he intended to propose to come to me as well, seeking guidance and also asking for confidentiality. Without revealing that I was counselling them both, I offered each the wisdom they sought, guiding them through this significant moment in their lives. When they eventually came together and discovered that I had been the confidant to both, they were amazed and grateful that I had managed to help them both without breaking their trust. It was a delicate dance, one that required careful navigation, but it underscored the importance of trust in relationships.

Life, as Michelle Obama wisely observed, is dynamic. "When they go low, we go high," she said, urging us to rise above the challenges and negativity that life throws our way. But she also added that when others go high, we must sometimes go low – remaining humble, grounded, and adaptable. In every situation, we are called to find the beauty, to draw out the good, even in the midst of trials. This is the essence of life – to live fully, to love deeply, and to remain resilient in the face of the inevitable ups and downs that define our days.

Happy Days Are Here to Stay

Happy days are here again

After the rain comes the flood

But the flood lasts for days, not forever

No matter how long it stays

We shall soon experience the drought

It's the normal cycle of life

To ride a bicycle

You must understand how a cycle works

The wheels are like a circle

Moving as you press the pedals

Strength is needed to keep pushing

Rusty and hard at first

But every push softens the wheel

Turning effort into smooth motion

Happy days are here again

After all the gloom

The air brims with the expectation of bloom

The hibiscus is ready to blossom

Its petals unfurling with vibrant grace

The cock, silent through the night

Now eager to announce the dawn

Its crow, loud and clear, cuts through the quiet

I thought I had seen it all

But wait, hope lingers in the air

The many expectations of the opponent fade away

Like shadows retreating from the morning sun

Optimism rises with each passing moment

A testament to the resilience of the spirit

Happy days are here to stay

A reminder that after every storm

The sky clears and the sun shines anew

In the cycle of struggle and relief

We find strength, growth, and renewal

Let us embrace these days with open hearts

For they bring the promise of brighter tomorrows

Happy Days Are Here to Stay

Life is not solely about the grey moments; sunshine always follows the rain. Happiness often mirrors the anticipation people feel on Fridays, knowing they have the freedom to enjoy themselves on Saturday. This feeling is beautifully captured in the popular phrase TGIF, or "Thank God it's Friday."

Throughout life, I have witnessed individuals face immense challenges. In those moments, it can seem as if their hopes and dreams may never come true. Yet, as the Bible reminds us:

"When the Lord brought back the captivity of Zion, we were like those who dream. Then our mouth was filled with laughter, and our tongue with singing. Then they said among the nations, 'The Lord has done great things for them.' The Lord has done great things for us, and we are glad. Bring back our captivity, O Lord, as the streams in the South. Those who sow in tears shall reap in joy. He who continually goes forth weeping, bearing seed for sowing, shall doubtless come again with rejoicing, bringing his sheaves with him." Psalms 126:1-6 (NKJV).

There was a day when the Lord turned the captivity of Zion, filling hearts with joy and gratitude. Just as they rejoiced, you too deserve happiness after everything you have endured. This is truly the day the Lord has made, and it is a time to be glad and celebrate.

Your journey to this point reflects incredible strength and resilience. Many who faced similar trials would not have the fortitude to persist as you have. There is a saying in my culture: "The eyes that have seen evil and are not blinded are about to witness good and rejoice."

Joy and expectation fill the air as things begin to turn in your favour. This is the moment you have been waiting for, so embrace and celebrate this remarkable time.

In the Jewish tradition, the Feast of Purim commemorates a time of deliverance and joy, as described in the Book of Esther:

"But the Jews who were at Shushan assembled together on the thirteenth day, as well as on the fourteenth; and on the fifteenth of the month, they rested, and made it a day of feasting and gladness. Therefore, the Jews of the villages who dwelt in the unwalled towns celebrated the fourteenth day of the month of Adar with gladness and feasting, as a holiday, and for sending presents to one another." Esther 9:18-19 (NKJV).

I believe your own season of celebration is here because things are turning in your favour. Consider what Mordecai, Esther, and the entire nation of Israel endured, and how their sorrow transformed into joy. It fills me with hope and joy to see the possibility of a divine turnaround in all areas of your life.

For me, this message serves as an encouragement after all I have experienced over the years – misunderstandings, disappointments, misrepresentations, losses, and other negative experiences. This is the turning point for me as well.

This joy and celebration are not fleeting; they are meant to last. "Weeping may endure for a night, but joy comes in the morning." I am filled with hope and gratitude to tell you that what you have been waiting for is finally here.

Personal Well-Being and Connection Worksheet

This worksheet is designed to help you strengthen connections with others and nurture your own well-being. Follow these steps to bring positivity and joy to yourself and those around you.

1. Reach Out to Others

Objective: Strengthen your relationships by showing care and concern for others.

Task: Call two or three people to check in on them.

- Choose Who to Call: Think of family members, friends, or colleagues you haven't spoken to in a while. Consider those who might appreciate some extra support or attention.
- Prepare Your Conversation:
- Start with a warm greeting and ask how they have been doing recently.
- Listen actively and offer empathy and support.
- Share some positive updates from your life and express your gratitude for having them in your life.
- Reflect on the Experience: After the call, take a moment to reflect on the conversation.

- Consider how it made you feel and how you might continue to nurture this relationship.

2. Send a Message of Hope

Objective: Communicate love and encouragement to your family.

Task: Send a heartfelt text message to your family members.

- Craft Your Message:
- Begin with a warm greeting and express your love and appreciation.
- Include a message of hope or encouragement that resonates with your family.
- Share a fond memory or something positive to look forward to in the future.
- Conclude with a reaffirmation of your support and affection.

Example Message:

"Hi [Family Member's Name], I just wanted to let you know how much I love and appreciate you. Despite the challenges we might face, I believe brighter days are ahead. Remember the time we [fond memory]? I'm looking forward to making more memories like that with you. Take care and know that I'm always here for you."

3. Treat Yourself

Objective: Practice self-care by indulging in something you enjoy.

Task: Buy or prepare a special meal you've been longing for.

- Plan Your Meal:
- Choose a dish that you have been craving. It could be a favourite comfort food or something new you've wanted to try.
- Decide whether you will prepare it yourself or order it from a restaurant.
- Enjoy the Experience:
- Set aside time to savour your meal without distractions. Consider creating a pleasant atmosphere with music or candles.
- Appreciate the flavours and the experience of treating yourself with kindness.
- Reflect on the Experience: Consider how treating yourself positively impacts your mood and energy levels.

4. Listen to Uplifting Music

Objective: Enhance your mood through music.

Task: Listen to a song or playlist that brings you joy.

- Select Your Music:
- Choose a song or playlist that makes you feel happy and relaxed. It could be a beloved classic,

a new favourite, or something recommended by a friend.

- Create a Listening Environment:
- Find a comfortable place to sit or lie down.
- Minimize distractions to fully immerse yourself in the music.
- Reflect on the Experience: Notice how the music affects your emotions and energy. Consider how you might incorporate music into your daily routine to boost your well-being.

5. Final Reflection:

After completing these activities, take a moment to reflect on how they have impacted your relationships and personal well-being. Consider how these practices can be integrated into your routine to maintain a positive and connected life.

www.ingramcontent.com/pod-product-compliance
Ingram Content Group UK Ltd.
Pitfield, Milton Keynes, MK11 3LW, UK
UKHW050247160425
457400UK00001B/1

9 781907 734564